# BLISS

# Pastoral

## LIE STREWN THE WHITE FLOCKS

for mezzo-soprano solo, SATB chorus, solo flute,
string orchestra & drums

*Poems selected from the works of Ben Johnson,*
*John Fletcher, Poliziano, Theocritus & Robert Nichols*

Order No: NOV070059

**NOVELLO PUBLISHING LIMITED**
14–15 Berners Street, London W1T 3LJ, UK

Time of Performance about 35 minutes

*By omitting "The Pigeon Song" the work can be performed with Choir and Orchestra only.*

Revised Reprint 1954

First Performance, London May 8 1929

**BY**

THE HAROLD BROOKE CHOIR

## THE SHEPHERD'S HOLYDAY

Thus, thus begin the yearly rites
Are due to Pan on these bright nights;
His morn now riseth and invites
To sports, to dances, and delights:
    All envious and profane, away,
    This is the shepherd's holyday.

Strew, strew the glad and smiling ground
With every flower, yet not confound:
The primrose drop, the spring's own spouse,
Bright day's-eyes and the lips of cows;
    The garden-star, the queen of May,
    The rose, to crown the holyday.

Drop, drop, you violets; change your hues,
Now red, now pale, as lovers use;
And in your death go out as well
As when you lived unto the smell:
    That from your odour all may say,
    This is the shepherd's holyday.

BEN JONSON (1573—1637)

## A HYMN TO PAN

All ye woods and trees, and bowers,
All ye virtues and ye powers
That inhabit in the lakes,
In the pleasant springs or brakes,
    Move your feet
      To our sound,
    Whilst we greet
      All this ground
With his honour and his name
That defends our flocks from blame.

He is great, and he is just,
He is ever good, and must
Thus be honour'd. Daffodillies,
Roses, pinks, and lovèd lilies,
    Let us fling,
    Whilst we sing,
    Ever holy,
    Ever holy,
Ever honour'd, ever young!
Thus great Pan is ever sung!

JOHN FLETCHER (1579-1625)

## PAN AND ECHO

Where while I seek you, Echo, do you lie, Love?
    I love!
Yes, and you love me say, none other—none?
    One!
You, you alone I love, for you there's no one else?
    One else!
Can you not say, " I love you, Pan, none other?"
    Another!
By this you tell me all my joy is sped?
    Dead!
Say his cursed name, that stole my love that throve!
    Love!
What shall he do that loved, that loved as I?
    Die!

POLIZIANO (1454-1494)

*Translated by E. Geoffrey Dunlop*

(By permission)

## THE NAIADS' MUSIC

*Naiads.*    Come, ye sorrowful, and steep
    Your tired brows in a nectarous sleep:
    For our kisses lightlier run
    Than the traceries of the sun
    By the lolling water cast
    Up grey precipices vast,
    Lifting smooth, and warm and steep
    Out of the palely shimmering deep.

*Fauns.**    I know a spot
    Where, to the sound of water sighing,
    The Naiads sing hushedly.

*Naiads.*    Come, ye sorrowful, and take
    Kisses that are but half awake:
    For here are eyes O softer far
    Than the blossom of the star
    Upon the mothy twilit waters,
    And here are mouths whose gentle
      laughters
    Are but the echoes of the deep
    Laughing and murmuring in its sleep.

*Fauns.*    I will repose
    Upon its banks and to the spring
    An answer make.

*Naiads.*    But if ye sons of Sorrow come
    Only wishing to be numb:
    Our eyes are sad as bluebell posies,
    Our breasts are soft as silken roses.
    And our hands are tenderer
    Than the breaths that scarce can stir
    The sunlit eglantine that is
    Murmurous with hidden bees.

*Fauns.*    Your deeps hold dreams
    Lovelier than sleep.

*Naiads.*    Come, ye sorrowful, for here
    No voices sound but fond and clear
    Of mouths as lorn as is the rose
    That under water doth disclose,
    Amid her crimson petals torn,
    A heart as golden as the morn;
    And here are tresses languorous
    As the weeds wander over us,
    And brows as holy and as bland
    As the honey-coloured sand
    Lying sun-entranced below
    The lazy water's limpid flow:
    Come, ye sorrowful, come!

*Fauns.*    Sweet watervoices! now must I
    Unto your sorrowings reply.

ROBERT NICHOLS

(By permission)

\* The words for the Fauns are selected from other parts of the poem.

## THE PIGEON SONG

Little pigeon, grave and fleet,
    Eye-of-fire, sweet Snowy-wings,
Think you that you can discover
    On what great green down my lover
Lies by his sunny sheep and sings?

If you can, O go and greet
    Him from me; say: She is waiting . . .
Not for him, O no! but, sweet,
    Say June's nigh and doves, remating,
Fill the dancing noontide heat
    With melodious debating.

Say the swift swoops from the beam ;
  Soon the cuckoo must cease calling ;
Kingcups flare beside the stream,
  That not glides now but runs brawling ;
That wet roses are asteam
  In the sun and will be falling.

Say the chestnut sheds his bloom ;
  Honey from straw hivings oozes ;
There's a night-jar in the coombe ;
  Venus nightly burns, and chooses
Most to blaze above my room ;
  That the laggard 'tis that loses.

Say the nights are warm and free,
  And the great stars swarm above him ;
But soon starless night must be.
  Yet if all these do not move him,
Tell, O tell—but not too plainly !—
  That I long for him and love him.

ROBERT NICHOLS

(By permission)

## THE SONG OF THE REAPERS†

Demeter, rich in fruit, and rich in grain, may this corn be easy to win, and fruitful exceedingly !

Bind, ye bandsters, the sheaves, lest the wayfarer should cry, Men of straw were the workers here, ay, and their hire was wasted !

See that the cut stubble faces the North wind, or the West ; 'tis thus the grain waxes richest.

They that thresh corn should shun the noonday sleep ; at noon the chaff parts easiest from the straw.

As for the reapers, let them begin when the crested lark is waking, and cease when he sleeps, but take holiday in the heat.

Boil the lentils better, thou miserly steward; take heed lest thou chop thy fingers, when thou'rt splitting cumin-seed.

THEOCRITUS

Translated by Andrew Lang

"The Lityerses Song,"from Andrew Lang's translation of Theocritus,
by permission of Macmillan & Co., Ltd.

# THE SHEPHERD'S NIGHT-SONG

Now arched dark boughs hang dim and still,
The deep dew glistens up the hill ;
Silence trembles. All is still.
Now the sweet siren of the woods,
Philomel, passionately broods,
Or, darkling, hymns love's wildest moods.
Danaë, fainting in her tower,
Feels a sudden sun swim lower,
Gasps beneath the starry shower.
Venus in the pomegranate grove
Flutters like a fluttering dove
Under young Adonis' love.
Leda longs until alight
In the reeds those wings of white
She hears beat the upper night.
Golden now the glowing moon,
Diana over Endymion
Downward bends as in a swoon.
Wherefore, since the gods agree
Youth is sweet and Night is free,
And Love pleasure, should not we ?

ROBERT NICHOLS

(By permission)

Shepherds all, and maidens fair,
Fold your flocks up, for the air
'Gins to thicken, and the sun
Already his great course hath run.
    Sweetest slumbers,
And soft silence, fall in numbers
On your eyelids ! So, farewell :
Thus I end my evening's knell.

JOHN FLETCHER (1579-1625)

[The poems by Robert Nichols are taken from " A Faun's Holiday " in the collection " Ardours and Endurances " published by Chatto and Windus (London) and Frederick A. Stokes Co. (New York), and are reprinted by permission.]

# PASTORAL "Lie strewn the white Flocks"

Arthur Bliss

# THE SHEPHERD'S HOLYDAY

**Ben Jonson (1573–1637)**

# A HYMN TO PAN

John Fletcher (1579—1625)

9

+*Original word 'greet'*

12

Ev - er hon - our'd,_____ ev - er young!_____

Ev - er hon - our'd,_____ ev - er young!

Ev - er hon - our'd,_____ ev - er young!_____

Ev - er hon - our'd,_____ ev - er young!_____

**24**

Thus great Pan is ev - er sung!_____

Thus great Pan is ev - er sung!_____

Thus great Pan is ev - er sung!_____

Thus great Pan is ev - er sung!_____

**24**

**25**

# PAN'S SARABAND

# PAN AND ECHO

Poliziano (1454—1494)
(tr. by E. Geoffrey Dunlop) *

# THE NAIADS' MUSIC

Robert Nichols[*]

Arthur Bliss

Copyright, 1929, by Novello & Company, Limited

24

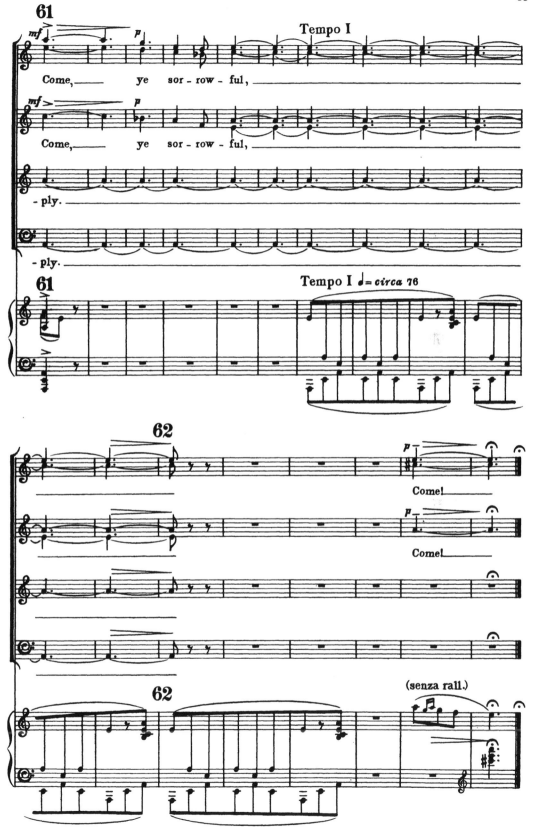

# THE PIGEON SONG

Robert Nichols*

*By permission

**65**

If you can, O go and greet Him from me; say:

*più mosso*

*mf* She is wait - ing—Not for him, O no! but, sweet,

*più mosso*

*mf*

**66**

*rall.*

Say June's nigh and doves, re-ma - ting, *rall.*

**Largamente**      **Tempo I**

*p* Fill the dancing noontide heat With me - lo - di - ous de - bat - ing.

**Largamente**      **Tempo I** ♪ = 88

Say the swift swoops from the beam; Soon the cuckoo must cease call-ing; King-cups flare be - side the stream, _____ That not glides now

38

(Violin)

sheds his bloom; Hon - ey from straw hiv - ings ooz - es; There's a night-jar in the

coombe; Ve-nus night - ly burns, and chooses Most to

blaze a - bove my room; That the lag - gard 'tis that

\* To be played by Flute when performed with Piano and Flute only

But soon star-less night must be.

quasi ad lib.

tenuto  Più animato

Yet  if all these do not move him,  Tell, O tell— but

tenuto  Più animato

not too plain - - ly! ——— That I long for

74 Largamente

him and love ——————————— him.

Largamente

a tempo (largamente)

molto rall.    rall.

Ah!

molto rall.   a tempo (largamente)   rall.

Theocritus
(tr. by Andrew Lang)*

# SONG OF THE REAPERS

may this corn be ea-sy to win, and fruit-ful ex-ceed-ing-ly!

may this corn be ea-sy to win, and fruit-ful ex-ceed-ing-ly!

may this corn be ea-sy to win, and fruit-ful ex-ceed-ing-ly!

may this corn be ea-sy to win, and fruit-ful ex-ceed-ing-ly!

# FINALE

See the heavy clouds low falling,
And bright Hesperus down calling
The dead Night from underground.
*Fletcher*

# THE SHEPHERD'S NIGHT SONG

Robert Nichols*

-til a - light In the reeds those wings of white __ She hears beat the up-per

-til a - light In the reeds those wings of white __ She hears beat the up-per

longs __ un - til those wings __ of white __ She

longs __ un - til those wings __ of white __ She

**97** a tempo

night. __ Gold-en now the

night. __ Gold-en now the

hears. __ Gold-en now the

hears. __ Gold-en now the

**97** dolce

glow-ing moon, __ Di - an - a o - ver En - dy-mi-on Downward bends as in a

glow-ing moon, __ Di - an - a o - ver En - dy-mi-on Downward bends as in a

glow-ing moon, __ Di - an - a o - ver En - dy-mi-on Downward bends as in a

glow-ing moon, __ Di - an - a o - ver En - dy-mi-on Downward bends as in a

And Love plea - sure, should not

And Love plea - sure, should not

should not

should not

we?

we?

we?

we?

Tempo dell Introduzione

**100**

Tempo dell Introduzione ♩ = 80

**100**

poco rall.

poco rall.

dolce

senza rall. *p

Shep-herds all, and maidens fair, Fold your

Shep-herds all, and maidens fair, Fold your

senza rall.

flocks up, for the air 'Gins to thick-en, and the sun Al-rea-dy his great

flocks up, for the air 'Gins to thick-en, and the sun Al-rea-dy his great

poco rit. **101** Pochissimo più mosso

course hath run._____ Sweet - est slum - bers,

Sweet - est slum - bers,

course hath run._____ Sweet - est slum - bers,

Sweet - est slum - bers,

poco rit. **101**

* From "The Faithful Shepherdess" — *Fletcher*